In the Bible, Jesus compared himself to a shepherd who had a hundred sheep. When one went missing, the shepherd was very upset! Even though he had 99 others, he wasn't happy until the lost lamb was back home safely. Jesus told this story so people would know how much each one of us means to God. God has a lot of children who love and obey Him, but when even just one of the people He made and loves gets carried away in sin, He is willing to do just about anything to reach them. Jesus was willing to go through the worst things you can think of, even die for you, so that you can be back at home in God's arms. If there is ever a time you feel lost and afraid, call out to Jesus. He always wants you back.

GOD IS HOLDING YOU

"MAY GOD'S DEAR ONE REST PEACEFULLY FOR GOD SHIELDS HIM ALL DAY LONG. GOD'S BELOVED CHILD SLEEPS LIKE A BABY ON HIS CHEST." DEUTERONOMY 33:12

YOU ARE SO LOVED

"GOD LOVES US SO MUCH THAT HE CALLS US HIS CHILDREN. HE IS OUR FATHER, IT IS REALLY TRUE!" 1 JOHN 3:1

GOD WANTS YOU

"GOD HAS CHOSEN YOU TO BE HIS SPECIAL TREASURE!"
DEUTERONOMY 14:2

YOU ARE INVITED

"JESUS SAID, 'MY FATHER'S HOUSE HAS MANY ROOMS AND I AM GOING THERE TO GET ONE READY FOR YOU SO THAT WE CAN ALWAYS BE TOGETHER AS A FAMILY.'" JOHN 14:2

GOD GIVES GREAT GIFTS

"All the best kinds of perfect gifts come from God." James 1:17

GOD CARES ABOUT YOU

"YOU CAN THROW YOUR PROBLEMS TO GOD. HE CARES FOR YOU AND IS HAPPY TO HANDLE THEM FOR YOU."
1 PETER 5:7

GOD ACCEPTS YOU

JESUS SAYS, "THE PERSON WHO COMES TO ME, I WILL NOT TURN AWAY!" JOHN 6:37

YOU ARE A BLESSING

"Children are a special treasure from God."

Psalm 127:3

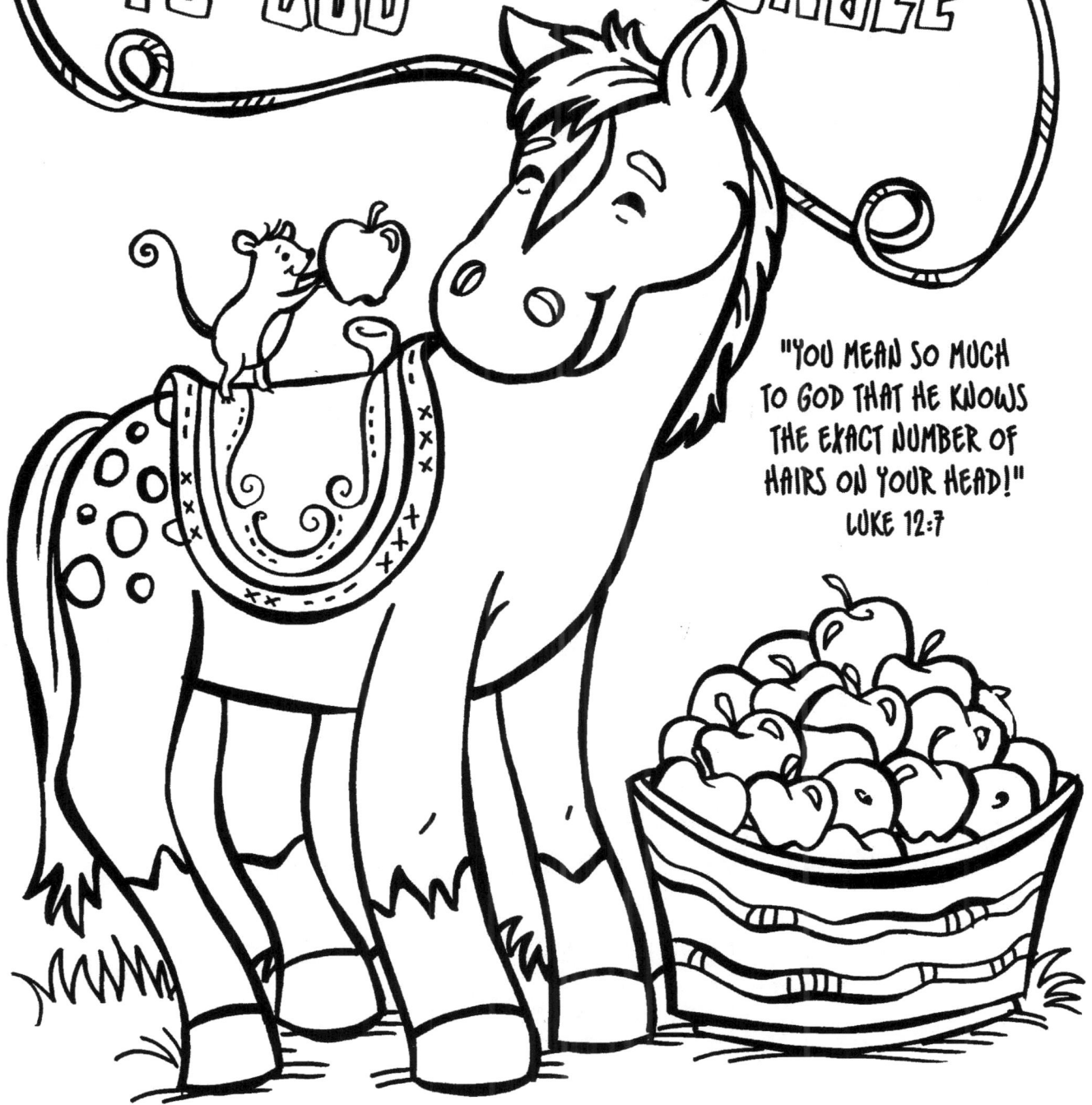

YOU ARE VALUABLE TO GOD

"YOU MEAN SO MUCH TO GOD THAT HE KNOWS THE EXACT NUMBER OF HAIRS ON YOUR HEAD!"
LUKE 12:7

YOU ARE UNFORGETTABLE

"GOD SAYS: 'NO WAY WOULD I EVER FORGET YOU! LOOK! I
HAVE YOUR NAME WRITTEN ON MY HAND!'"
ISAIAH 49:15

GOD IS SHAPING YOUR LIFE

"GOD, YOU ARE OUR FATHER. YOU SHAPE US LIKE A POTTER SHAPES CLAY."
ISAIAH 64:8

GOD IS GIVING

"GOD DOESN'T HOLD BACK GOOD THINGS FROM HIS CHILDREN." PSALM 84:11

YOU CAN
RELY
ON GOD

"THE ETERNAL GOD IS
YOUR REFUGE, AND
UNDERNEATH ARE THE
EVERLASTING ARMS!"
DEUTERONOMY 33:27

YOU ARE PART OF GODS FAMILY

"GOD PLACES THE LONELY IN FAMILIES! HE SETS THE PRISONERS FREE AND GIVES THEM JOY!" PSALM 68:6

GOD SINGS FOR YOU

"God delights over you with a happy song."
Zephaniah 3:17

GOD FORGIVES

"IF WE TELL GOD WE ARE SORRY WHEN WE SIN, AND WE TRULY MEAN IT, HE WILL DEFINITELY FORGIVE US EVERY TIME! THAT IS JUST HOW GOOD HE IS!"
1 JOHN 1:9

YOU CAN CHANGE

"GOD SAYS FROM HIS HEAVENLY THRONE:
'I MAKE ALL THINGS NEW!'"
REVELATION 21:5

YIPPPEE!

"It is party time in Heaven whenever a lost
person turns back from wrong doing
and runs toward God!"
Luke 15:7

GOD CHEERS FOR YOU

"GOD IS DELIGHTED WITH YOU! HE WILL KEEP YOU CALM WITH HIS LOVE.
HE WILL SING FOR JOY OVER YOU!" ZEPHANIAH 3:17

"God says, 'Even to your OLD AGE and GRAY HAIR I will carry you, I will take care of you, and I will rescue you!"

Isaiah 46:4

GOD BLESS YOU OVER AND OVER

"MAY THE LORD BLESS YOU AND KEEP YOU SAFE. MAY GOD SMILE
ON YOU AND BE KIND TO YOU. MAY HE SHOW YOU HOW SPECIAL
YOU ARE TO HIM AND GIVE YOU HIS PEACE."
NUMBERS 6:24-26

YOU CAN SHARE IT

"I will never hide the good news about Jesus!
It is the power of God to save people!"
Romans 1:16

NAME CATS

"God says, 'I could never forget you! I have your name written on my hand!" Isaiah 49:15

FINISH THE PUPPY

"God started something good in you and He will finish it!" Philippians 1:6

DESIGN A SWEATER FOR THIS CHILLY DOG

"You are God's beloved child! So look like Him by wearing His kind of compassion, kindness, humility, gentleness and patience."
Colossians 3:10

DECORATE THE CAKE

"See for yourself how sweet God is!" Psalm 34:8

DESIGN HER DRESS

"Christ gave His own life for you, the way a husband defends his bride." Ephesians 5:27

DESIGN HIS SUPERSUIT

"You can do anything if you rely on Jesus to give you extra super-strength from on high!" Philippians 4:13

ADD FACIAL HAIR

"This is how much God cares for you:
He knows how many hairs are on your
head!" Matthew 10:30

DRAW THE FRUIT

"When God lives in your life, He
makes these qualities grow in you like fruit on a tree:
Love, joy, peace, patience, kindness, goodness, faithfulness
gentleness and self control. They just come naturally!" Galatians 5:22-23

HERE, KITTY KITTY...

1

2

3

4

5

YOU ARE GETTING VERY HUNGRY!

1

2

3

4

5

6

TRY THIS

1. Start with the head!

2. Add a face, neck, and back.

3. Legs and belly!

4. Finish off with a tail, mane and bridle. Saddle up! Yeehaw!

AND THIS

1. Doggy head.

Add some freckles →

3. Add front legs and back.

Show a hint of ear on the back side of head. →

2. Add face, tongue and collar.

4. Finish off by adding a back leg and paw. Add a tail, some toes, and spots! Fido is ready to fetch!

FINISH THE PICTURE

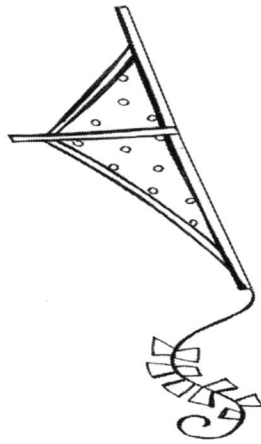

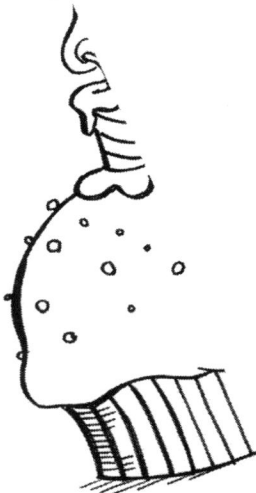

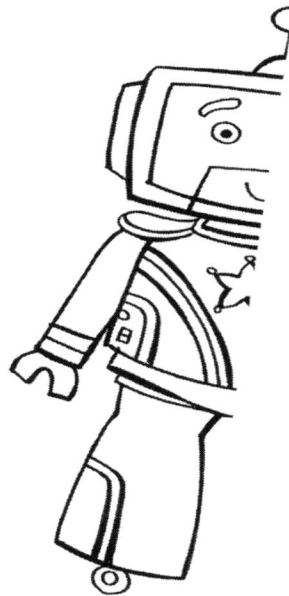

"GOD LOVES US MORE THAN YOU CAN IMAGINE--
SO MUCH, THAT HE GAVE WHAT MEANT MOST TO HIM.
GOD GAVE HIS ONE AND ONLY SON, JESUS, AND ANYONE
WHO TRULY BELIEVES IN HIM WILL NOT DIE BUT
HAVE LIFE ETERNAL!"
JOHN 3:16

Made in the USA
Las Vegas, NV
17 September 2022

55477625R00024